To Nancy

God Bless You

Pastor A.G. Miller

ENJOY YOUR JOURNEY

DR. ALYN E. WALLER

ENJOY YOUR JOURNEY

*Our Quest for a Deeper
Relationship with Christ*

CLC
PUBLICATIONS
Fort Washington, PA 19034

Published by CLC ❖ Publications

U.S.A.
P.O. Box 1449, Fort Washington, PA 19034

GREAT BRITAIN
51 The Dean, Alresford, Hants. SO24 9BJ

AUSTRALIA
P.O. Box 213, Bungalow, Cairns, QLD 4870

NEW ZEALAND
10 MacArthur Street, Feilding

ISBN 0-87508-824-4

Table of Contents

Foreword

Every once in a while a gallant thinker takes on the challenge of finding meaning in this thing we call life. It is no secret that life raises more questions than it does answers and as one philosopher concluded, "Life is not a question to be solved but a mystery to be experienced." Alyn Waller takes up the challenge to not only journey through the experience but to also find principles and precepts to guide us along the way.

Enjoy Your Journey is a refreshing look at the wilderness journey of the children of Israel and the journey of a deepening relationship with Christ. Alyn Waller sees Israel's experience as clear truth with powerful revelation. We are not created to fatalistically accept our time; rather, we are called to live joyfully and enthusiastically through every situation and every challenge. God is calling us to find joy in the journey.

In a time of great pessimism and uncertainty, this work calls us to reconsider how we view our days and calls us to find the hope, the joy, the excitement, and the power of God that is available for the journey that is inevitably ours to make. It offers hope for the weary traveler and light for those who are struggling with the darkness. The old spiritual says, "Lord how come me here?" and this work makes as its aim giving all who ask the question a heads up on the answer. Each page shakes the foundations of human despair until we too reach the conclusion that we are to *fear God and keep His commands.*

Bishop Walter Scott Thomas
Pastor, New Psalmist Baptist Church
Prelate of the Kingdom Association of Covenant Pastors

Preface

This small book is based on a series of sermons I have shared with our church family. This series is a reminder to all of us that life is a journey of ins and outs, ups and downs, appointments and disappointments; however, it is a journey that God intends for us to enjoy.

To my wife, Ellyn: Thank you for your support and for your prayers and most of all thank you for sharing this journey with me.

To my daughters, Eryka and Morgan: You are my inspiration; you have made, and continue to make, my journey a joy.

To my mother, Belva Waller, and in memory of my father, the Rev. Dr. Alfred M. Waller: Thank you for starting my journey and pushing me to my destiny.

To the Enon Tabernacle Baptist Church: Our journey together is really just beginning. Although we have already experienced much, the best is yet to come.

Alyn Waller

ENJOY YOUR JOURNEY

To everything there is a season,
a time for every purpose under heaven.

A time to be born, and a time to die;
A time to plant, and a time to pluck what is planted;

A time to kill, and a time to heal;
A time to break down, and a time to build up;

A time to weep, and a time to laugh;
A time to mourn, and a time to dance;

A time to cast away stones, and a time to gather stones;
A time to embrace, and a time to refrain from embracing;

A time to gain, and a time to lose;
A time to keep, and a time to throw away;

A time to tear, and a time to sew;
A time to keep silence, and a time to speak;

A time to love, and a time to hate;
A time of war, and a time of peace.

What profit has the worker from that in which he labors?
I have seen the God-given task with which
sons of men are to be occupied.
He has made everything beautiful in its time.
Also He has put eternity in their hearts,
except that no one can find out the
work that God does from beginning to end.

I know that there is nothing better for them than to rejoice,
and to do good in their lives, and also that every man should
eat and enjoy the good of all his labor—it is the gift of God.

Ecclesiastes 3:1–13 (NKJV)

ONE

The Seasons of Life

An ancient maze-like pattern called the labyrinth has been used for centuries by Christians and non-Christians alike as a meditational device. The most well-known labyrinth is found at Chartres Cathedral in France. It is a series of curved pathways; you begin on the outside and walk to the center, then walk back out. As you walk the labyrinth, you pray and meditate. Many people have reported that as they have walked the labyrinth they have had visions or received answers to their problems. It is a very interesting practice.

There are many Christian churches that use the labyrinth as a meditational device. There are evangelical groups that have developed a procedure of walking a labyrinth that is specifically Christ-centered. Some believers are concerned that this practice is syncretistic—that Christians should not use this because of its pagan connections. It is a religious tradition that predates Christianity, and there is the potential for those who practice it to place more emphasis on the walk than on the One to whom they are praying. Whatever you believe about this tradition, one thing that makes walking a labyrinth so powerful is that it is a strong metaphor for the reality that *life is a journey*.

Life Is a Journey

Life is not a series of *non-sequiturs*, not a bunch of unrelated happenings. You are on a journey, and as soon as you realize that, you will have a whole new perspective on your present situation.

Once you realize that you are on a journey, life begins to take on new meaning. When you begin to accept that all things have purpose, and that experiences come and go in our lives for a reason, you can learn how to say, "This too will pass." I have learned to ask myself, "What can I learn from this experience?" I have become more patient with others, knowing that since I am on a journey others must be on journeys as well. Since I am not the author of my journey or the journey of anyone else, I cannot be judgmental about where others are on their journey. Maybe we are on similar journeys but at different points along our way, and so, instead of being judgmental, maybe I ought to encourage others along the way.

Recognizing life as a journey helps me to avoid getting stuck in any particular moment of life. I can enjoy the moment, but I shouldn't get stuck in the moment. I can hate the moment, but I should not let the moment define me forever. It is God's intention that you enjoy your journey; you really are supposed to enjoy life. There is something wrong with always being angry and always being distressed. If you let everything that happens to you rock your world, you are in for a rocky existence! Bless God, even in difficult times. Doing this is possible only if we understand that we are on a journey, and the journey is the will of God for our lives.

The book of Ecclesiastes helps me to understand life as a journey. Ecclesiastes 3:1–12 is a passage of Scripture that even many non-Christians have heard before. It says,

To everything there is a season, a time for every purpose
    under heaven:
A time to be born, and a time to die;
    a time to plant, and a time to pluck what is planted;
A time to kill, and a time to heal;
    a time to break down, and a time to build up;
A time to weep, and a time to laugh;
    a time to mourn, and a time to dance;
A time to cast away stones, and a time to gather stones;
    a time to embrace, and a time to refrain from embrac-
    ing;
A time to gain, and a time to lose;
    a time to keep, and a time to throw away;
A time to tear, and a time to sew;
    a time to keep silence, and a time to speak;
A time to love, and a time to hate;
    a time of war, and a time of peace.

What profit has the worker from that in which he labors? I have seen the God-given task with which the sons of men are to be occupied. He has made everything beautiful in its time. Also He has put eternity in their hearts, except that no one can find out the work that God does from beginning to end.

I know that there is nothing better for them than to rejoice, and to do good in their lives.

Solomon is the traditionally agreed-upon author of the book of Ecclesiastes. His authorship does raise a question in my mind, however. The eleventh chapter of First Kings says that Solomon did evil in the sight of the Lord in his later years. Why would God allow the wisdom of someone who did evil in His sight to be included in the Bible?

When you read Ecclesiastes, it seems to ring of pessimism and cynicism. It almost reads as if Jerry Seinfeld wrote the book! Solomon says things like, "What happens to the man who works hard all his life? And what happens to the man who doesn't work hard at all? They both die." He writes things like, "The race isn't given to the swift or the battle to the strong," and we add, "but to those that endure to the end." But when he wrote it, what he really meant was, "Life doesn't make sense—the fastest person doesn't win the race; the strongest person doesn't win the fight. All is vanity; everything is meaningless." In a sense, Solomon is saying that nothing is worth living for; nothing is worth doing.

When you read Ecclesiastes, it seems to ring of pessimism and cynicism.

Solomon concludes the book by saying, "Just trust in God." Solomon is saying to us, "If there is anything you can learn from my life, it is this: don't get caught up in the various moments of your life. Life is a compilation of good and bad experiences that do not always immediately make sense, but if we trust in God, all of life's experiences work together to accomplish God's will for our lives."

I can understand how Solomon became such a cynic. Solomon was a politician. He tried to possess the international influence that his father David enjoyed, but he was not as charismatic as David. So Solomon used shrewd political alliances to extend the borders of his people. That's why Solomon had so many wives; when Solomon made a treaty with another country, that country would give him wives to seal the deal. Solomon had acquired many wives due to all of the political schemes with the countries around him.

> *When you play politics all your life—tricking and scheming to make life happen instead of allowing the will of God to take place in your life—life can wear you out.*

When you play politics all your life—tricking and scheming to make life happen instead of allowing the will of God to take place in your life—life can wear you out. So Solomon says, "Don't get caught up in what you want to do and in what happens to you; don't get so hurried that you miss the blessing of the day. Just trust in God and enjoy your journey."

The third chapter begins, "To everything there is a season, a time for every purpose under heaven." Our lives are built around seasons—seasons of sorrow and seasons of joy, good times and bad times, easy roads and difficult roads.

Some of us may find it difficult to read lines like "a time to hate" and "a time to kill," but Solomon is not writing a prescription (how things should be, or how we are supposed to live our lives), but a description (how things are in the real world, whether we like it or not). Solomon has lived a long time and has learned many things. He is describing what happens in life—for example, there are times of war and times of peace. Solomon wasn't suggesting that war is a good thing, nor is it something we ought to seek after; he is simply acknowledging that it happens.

This list of occurrences can happen in any of our lives. Yes, even "tongue-talking super-saints" can experience trouble. Far too many Christians run into hard times and are so quick to say, "Why me?" And we get stuck right there. The real question should be, "Why not me?" What's so special about any of us that no hurt or harm should ever come our way?

God loves and cares for you. But in the context of His providence and permissive will, He sometimes allows trouble to come into your life. The reality is that even out of trouble He can produce character in you. You see, God is working on this thing called *you*, and it takes your mother and father, your formal and informal education, good times and bad times, sunshine and rain to make this thing called *you*. There is a gap between where you are and where God wants you to be, and getting you there is going to include some good stuff and some challenging stuff. Let me see if I can make this plain.

> *There is a gap between where you are and where God wants you to be, and getting you there is going to include some challenging stuff.*

One Sunday morning I had an interesting conversation with my coffee cup. I was drinking coffee at about 5:30 a.m. and my cup looked up at me and said, "Alyn, I know that you are going to be preaching from Ecclesiastes this morning and I want you to share with the body of Christ my testimony."

I asked, "What can you tell me, Coffee Cup, that will help my congregation understand this journey?"

It replied, "Alyn, you like me, don't you?"

I said, "I sure do, Coffee Cup. I drink coffee out of you every morning and I like your design. You really are useful to me."

The coffee cup then said, "Well, Alyn, let me share

my story with you. I have not always been what I am right now. A few years ago I was just a lump of clay. Then a man picked me up and put me on a table. The table starting spinning, and I didn't know what was going on. I said, 'Wait a minute!' And he said, 'I am not finished with you yet,' and then I couldn't believe it—he punched me and smashed me and it really hurt.

"I said, 'Get your hands off me!' But he said, 'I am not done with you yet.' And then he molded me and smoothed me out. The next thing he did was he started painting me. I have to admit, the paintbrush felt good. I started looking good, and I began thinking that maybe the worst part was over—but then he put me in an oven! It was hot in there, and I cried, 'Let me out! Let me out!' But he said, 'I am not done with you yet.'

There is a lesson in every moment. And going on to the next level depends on learning the lesson from the previous level.

"Finally he brought me out of the oven, and all of a sudden I was different. He put me in a store and they placed a price tag on me. Then you came along, Alyn. You paid for me and brought me home. I wasn't worth much when that man picked me up as a small lump of clay, but now that I've been through a few things, I am useful."

You may feel like your life has spun out of control, like you've had a hole punched in you and been thrown into the oven; but know that God is making something beautiful out of you. That's the journey! Understanding life as a journey requires learning some of life's lessons along the way.

Life's Lessons

There is a lesson in every moment. Going on to the next level depends upon learning the lesson from the previous level. A well-known behavioral scientist by the name of Erik Erikson spoke of human development in eight stages. The degree to which we successfully navigate each stage increases the probability that we will handle future stages successfully. This example in the natural realm helps me to understand how God deals with us in the spiritual realm. In other words, if you don't pass the test or learn the lesson where you are now, then you will not be able to handle the next stage that God has for you.

You may be looking back, thinking about yesterday, or looking ahead, already worrying about tomorrow.

You must learn to say, "If God has allowed this thing to happen in my life, there must be something I can learn from it." The Word of God tells us that "all things work together for good to those who love God, to those who are the called according to His purpose" (Rom. 8:28). We don't learn the lesson by asking why, but by giving thanks in all things. "In everything give thanks; for this is the will of God in Christ Jesus for you" (1 Thess. 5:18).

I don't get into a situation and begin to pity myself. I begin to thank God, because my attitude in my situation will determine how and what I get out of my situation. I like how Joyce Meyer puts it: "I can complain and remain, or I can praise and be raised!"

You need to thank God in the midst of your troubles. If you are going to learn your lesson, you have to be present for your promotion. Many of us never move to the next level because we are not present in our pain. You may be looking back, thinking about yesterday, or looking ahead, already worrying about tomorrow. You are not present in the moment to either feel the pain or enjoy the moment. And then you never move on from that moment. Let me make this plain.

When I was in the tenth grade—I am not proud of this—I flunked two classes and had to go to summer school. Summer school in any public school is never pleasant, because public schools in the North don't have air conditioning (at least they didn't back in the '70s!). While all my friends were out swimming, playing ball and having a good time, there I was, literally sweating it out in summer school. My friends were talking about eleventh grade, but I couldn't get eleventh grade out of my mouth, because I was in summer school. I was trying to learn the things I should have learned back in the spring, but because I wasn't present, attentive, or studious, I never got out of it what I should have, so I had to go to summer school.

You may be wondering right now why you can't move on in life. Maybe it's because you are trying to avoid the pain, trying to avoid learning the lesson where you are. God has you in spiritual summer school. And until you learn the lesson, until you learn to appreciate and praise God in the midst of where you are, you can't move on to the next season of your life.

Some Christians get stuck and allow the worst times of their lives to define them, or the best days of their lives to define them.

I encourage you to start thanking God for whatever is going on in your life. I dare you to start saying, "Hallelujah, anyhow!" I dare you to take God at His word and watch how the lessons of life begin to open up. To learn the lessons of our lives, we have to be present in the moment. Don't let one season define your whole life.

Seasons Do End

Ecclesiastes 3 teaches us that we need to move on from one season to the next—a time to be born, a time to die; a time to plant and a time to pluck what is planted; a time to kill and a time to heal; a time to break down and a time to build up. You need to move on. You can't get stuck in either the mountains or the valleys of your life. Some Christians get stuck and allow the worst times of their lives to define them, or the best days of their lives to define them.

One month before he was killed, Martin Luther King, Jr. preached a wonderful, prophetic sermon entitled "Unfulfilled Dreams." This sermon is recorded in the book *A Knock at Midnight*,[1] an anthology of his sermons. Preaching at his home church, he said, "When I die, I don't want you to remember me for either the mountaintop experiences or the dark valleys." The basic message in this sermon was, in essence, "I've done some great things, I've been a part of a major move in America, but I have also made some mistakes." Dr. King basically said, "Don't let one moment be the definition of who I am—let the sum total of my life speak for itself." If Dr. Martin Luther King, Jr., one of the greatest and most influential voices of the 20th century, could put his life in that type of perspective, certainly you and I should learn to do the same.

You are more than one season of your life. If you can't move forward, maybe it's because you are still allowing bad things from your past to define who you are. Maybe you were in jail, but you are not in jail any longer. America might not let it go, but you can. Maybe you have been through a bad divorce, but that does not have to define the rest of your life. You are not used goods. Maybe you were strung out on drugs, but you are clean today! And now you can move forward. Maybe it has been difficult for you, but God has already forgiven what you can't seem to forget. Don't allow yourself to be stuck in a past season.

Do not allow any season of your life to define you, and don't let others define you by the seasons of your life.

There is another side to this. Never allow yourself to be defined by the highest moment of your life either. You might be someone that the Lord used mightily at another time in your life, yet you are living as if it were yesterday. I do not mean to demean or downplay the wonderful ways God has used you, but even that is over now. It is part of your résumé, but remember that what you do is not who you are. Even more importantly, you need to remember that you are neither the best thing in your life nor the worst thing in your life. Do not allow any season of your life to define you, and don't let others define you by the seasons of your life.

Paul said, "I have learned in whatever state I am, to be content" (Phil. 4:11). What he was saying was "I've learned how to handle the various seasons of my life, and to rejoice in all of it!" Paul told the Philippians that he was waiting on the financial help that they were going to send, but it was delayed. However, God used that moment in Paul's life to teach him "how to be abased and . . . how to abound" (4:12). He was saying, "I've learned how to be happy when I have everything I need, and also when I don't have everything I need." God orchestrated a low moment in Paul's life, not to define him in that moment, but to teach him how God can take care of him when others fail. So Paul could say, "I can do all things through Christ who strengthens me" (4:13). Why? Because "my God shall supply all your need according to His riches in glory" (4:19).

This is the same Paul who, in Acts 28, on the island of Malta, did not allow people's definition of him to define him. He was putting wood on the fire, and a poisonous snake jumped out of the pile of sticks he had put on the fire and bit him. The people said, "He must be a murderer"—they thought that because they believed bad things happen to bad people. But when he shook the snake off and he didn't die, the same people said, "He is a god" (28:3–6). People will always say you are better or worse than you really are. And if you allow people to define who you are based on what happens in your life, you are in for a tumultuous existence.

Punctuate Them with a Praise

I am not my highest moment nor am I my lowest moment, and I am definitely not who others say I am. Who I am is *who I am in God*. If you know that, you can praise God for the bad things in your past as well as the good, without getting caught up in any of it. If you really want to get out of life all that you can, learn how to punctuate every season with a praise.

> *It has gotten so that when I see trouble coming in my life, I've learned to praise Him even before I get into the trouble.*

In Ecclesiastes 3, Solomon decides that the only thing that really matters in life is to do good and rejoice. In other words, whatever I go through, I can come out of it praising God for what I went through—because I know that I am on a journey. And if I am on a journey, that means God led me this way. And if God led me *to* this, God will lead me *through* this. There must be something I needed to learn from it. I can come out of this with something new that I have learned about God and myself, and then I will be ready for the next season of my life.

I've learned how to praise God when I am on the mountain, but more importantly, I've learned how to praise God in the midst of my struggle. It has gotten so that when I see trouble coming in my life, I've learned to praise Him even before I get in the trouble. Because when trouble comes my way, that just tells me that God is getting ready to launch a new thing in my life. When I see things coming my way that I know I can't handle, that just means that God is getting ready to teach me something new.

I've learned how to say, "Hallelujah, anyhow!"

So I praise Him and thank Him for my mountains and for my valleys, because I know He has not brought me this far to leave me. Hallelujah! I am going to bless the Lord. I am going to hold His hand. I am going to praise Him on the way in and on the way out. I am going to enjoy my journey. When I am going through the ups and downs of life, in order to learn my lesson and move on I hold onto the truth of this psalm:

> The LORD is my light and my salvation; whom shall I fear? The LORD is the strength of my life; of whom shall I be afraid? When the wicked came against me to eat up my flesh, my enemies and foes, they stumbled and fell. Though an army may encamp

against me, my heart shall not fear; though war may rise against me, in this will I be confident.

One thing I have desired of the LORD, that will I seek: that I may dwell in the house of the LORD all the days of my life, to behold the beauty[a] of the LORD, and to inquire in His temple. For in the time of trouble He shall hide me in His pavilion; in the secret place of His tabernacle He shall hide me; He shall set me high upon a rock.

And now my head shall be lifted up above my enemies all around me; therefore I will offer sacrifices of joy[b] in His tabernacle; I will sing, yes, I will sing praises to the LORD. Hear, O LORD, when I cry with my voice! Have mercy also upon me, and answer me. When You said, "Seek My face," my heart said to You, "Your face, LORD, I will seek." Do not hide Your face from me; do not turn Your servant away in anger; You have been my help; do not leave me nor forsake me, O God of my salvation. When my father and my mother forsake me, then the LORD will take care of me.

Teach me Your way, O LORD, and lead me in a smooth path, because of my enemies. Do not deliver me to the will of my adversaries; for false witnesses have risen against me, and such as breathe out violence. I would have lost heart, unless I had believed that I would see the goodness of the LORD in the land of the living.

Wait on the LORD; be of good courage, and He shall strengthen your heart; wait, I say, on the LORD. (Psalm 27)

---

a. *the beauty*: or, *the delight*.
b. *joy*: Heb. *shouting*.

Discussion Questions

1. How is the Christian life like a journey? How does it help us to think of it that way?
2. Have you ever felt "stuck" at a certain level? What needs to be done to move on?
3. Do you ever feel like others define you by a certain season in your life? Do you ever do that yourself? What do you do to get past that?
4. What does the author mean when he says to "punctuate with praise" the seasons of life? How do you praise God when you don't "feel" like it?

Key Verses

Ecclesiastes 3:1–12   Philippians 4:11–13, 19
Psalm 27:3–5   1 Thessalonians 5:18
Romans 8:28

Two

From Visitation to Habitation

And he [Moses] said, "Please, show me Your glory."
(Ex. 33:18)

If there is one thing that bothers a mother more than anything else, it is to see her son, whom she has raised to be a man, acting like a boy. If you want to see my mother get mad, just let her catch me behaving in a way which, to her, does not seem appropriate for the man she intended me to grow into. I may be forty-one years old now, but any kind of immature behavior on my part still makes her mad. I mean, she really gets irate, along with my wife—and then the two of them gang up on me!

A mother invests a lot of time in a son, and she wants him to grow up and be a man. A healthy mother doesn't want you to become a mama's boy; she releases you into manhood. And she doesn't begin when you are twenty-one—she begins when you are born. Real parenting begins at birth, and even at twelve months a good parent begins to teach lessons of maturity, such as delayed gratification and treating other people with consideration.

When I was a little boy I used to hide behind my mother when someone would speak to me. You know what I mean—when you are two or three years old and you are shy, you don't really want to deal with people, so you just hide behind your mother and look out at them from behind her skirt. That was how I treated other people, and it worked—for a while. But as I got older, I can remember my mother giving me signs that things weren't going to be like they used to be. I tried to hide behind her when I was five and she gently pushed me from behind her and said, "You're too big for that now."

When I was a little child, maybe about two or

three years old, I would run to my mother and jump into her arms, and she would catch me. I tried that when I was five and she just said kindly, "You are too big for that." I couldn't continue to jump into her arms the rest of my life. I couldn't hide behind her forever. I was getting too big for that. These things bothered me at the time and it seemed to me that my mother was being mean; however, the reality was she was maturing me for my journey.

Growing Up in God

This is a lesson that we all have to learn as we grow in God. As we walk with the Lord we will enter new seasons in our lives in which God will remind us, "You are getting too big for that; I want to move you into a new season of maturity." God is saying to us, "You're getting too big for some of the stuff you've been doing." You're too big to just want "Holy Ghost Happy Hour." It's time to want more of God. You're too big to simply go through the motions of religiosity. It's time to go deeper in God. You're too big to come to church only for what you can get out of it. It's time to start seeking God's face and not just His hands. It's

> *It's time to start seeking God's face and not just His hands. It's time to move from visitation to habitation.*

time to move from visitation to habitation.

Our mothers wanted us to grow up, to become mature. And God also requires us to go on to maturity. This is not just physical or social maturity, but spiritual maturity. Spiritual maturity is that point in your relationship with God in which you realize that you don't know everything; you acknowledge that life is a journey, and you understand that God is an eternal partner in this journey.

Spiritual maturity is that point in your walk with God that you don't need your flesh tickled. You don't need the proof of miracles or the aid of signs and wonders to maintain your faith in God. God may perform signs and wonders early on in your Christian life, to show you who God is. And while those are valid parts of our experience, at some point you ought not need that to maintain your faith in God. At some point you have to know that God is present, whether there is a burning bush or not.

Spiritual maturity is that point in your walk with God that you don't need your flesh tickled.

For far too many of us, our faith in God is so flimsy that it rests on somebody else's life. By that I mean that you love God until somebody makes you mad or until an unfortunate experience comes into your life

—then all of a sudden you don't want to go to church anymore. You believe in God until some church leader fails to live up to your expectations, then all of a sudden your faith has been shaken. But at some point you have to have a faith in God that stands—even if you run into people whose character and conduct are not becoming of their profession of faith. You have to grow to a point where you can say, "I know who God is; you can't make me doubt Him because I know Him for myself."

Spiritual maturity is that place in God where you are moving past the simple questions of faith, as it says in Hebrews 6:1–2: "Therefore, leaving the discussion of the elementary principles of Christ, let us go on to perfection, not laying again the foundation of repentance from dead works and of faith toward God, of the doctrine of baptisms, of laying on of hands, of resurrection of the dead, and of eternal judgment." In other words, at some point I've got to say that I am settled in my salvation.

Spiritual maturity says, "I am ready to go deeper into the things of God . . ."

Spiritual maturity has to do with settling in with God for the long haul and realizing that there is so much to God that it is going to take all of my life and the life hereafter to plumb the depths of who God really is. Spiritual maturity says, "I am ready to go deeper into the things of God and to the next level of practical victorious Christian living that God has for me." God does not want you to just walk down the aisle, join a church and sit there in the pew, without ever growing in Him. There is so much more to life with God than just joining a church. God wants you to go deeper in Him and learn all that He has for you and wants to do in you, through you, and with you. It is time for us to move from visitation to habitation.

Going Deeper with God

"From visitation to habitation" is the phrase that Tommy Tenney uses in the book *The God Chasers*[2] when he tells the story of Moses on the mountain. Moses is essentially saying to God, "I want to go deeper in You. I want to move from simply having experiences of You to having a relationship with You, so that You are with me all the time. I want to begin to know more and more about who You are." This is moving from visitation to habitation.

> *The real proof that you have the Holy Spirit in your life is* not *how high you jump on Sunday.*

It is more than just Jesus on Sunday morning. It is taking the name of Jesus with you when you leave church. The real proof that you have the Holy Spirit in your life is not how high you jump on Sunday. I don't mind jumping on Sunday, but the real evidence of the anointing of the Holy Spirit in your life is how you walk on Monday. Moving from visitation to habitation means saying to God, "Lord, I want to go as deep into You as You will allow me; I want You to do with me as You please." In other words, you have to surrender everything to God.

This is the deeper meaning behind the saying that God is not interested in your ability but your availability. God can do extraordinary things through ordinary people—if they surrender themselves. God wants to use you, but He can't when you are in the driver's seat. You may say, "God is my copilot," but God says, "If I'm not driving, I'm not riding!'"

Many Christians never move on into the deep things of God because they won't let go of the wheel. And if they give God the wheel, they keep their foot on the brake. But if you really want to move deeper in God, you've got to surrender yourself to Him.

And this was the point Moses had come to when he said to God, "Show me Your glory." By this time he'd had a lot of experiences with God. He had seen the burning bush that was not consumed, and the miracles in Egypt; he had watched God part the Red Sea, gotten manna from on high, and had a number of conversations with God on the mountain and in the tent of meeting. He had been protected by God with a cloud during the day and a fire by night. Moses had even made some mistakes, but God had forgiven him and taken him back. Moses had gone a long way with God, and yet Moses said, "God, I know that there is more to You and I want to go deeper in You."

> *Moses had gone a long way with God, and yet Moses said, "God, I know that there is more to You and I want to go deeper in You."*

A real relationship with God is not just about getting things from God; it's about having God with you. And that's what Moses was saying on the mountain. In Exodus 33, Moses says to God, "If You don't go with us, I don't want to go." In fact, God's presence is what differentiated the people of Israel from the peoples around them—not just God's stuff, but His presence. I don't know about you, but I want to feel God's presence in my life. I want people to perceive that the Lord is with me. That's what it means to move from visitation to habitation.

A Hunger for Holiness

How do we move from visitation to habitation? Well, first you need a hunger for holiness. When Moses said, "Please, show me Your glory," he was saying, "I need more of You, God. I want to go past these experiences with You and get right in Your face. Show me Your glory." This is the second time that Moses was on the mountain receiving the law from God. The first time he received the law, he came down the mountain and discovered that the children of Israel had turned away from God and had made a golden calf. Moses broke the tablets of the law in the process of destroying the golden calf.

This time when he comes up the mountain he says to God, "I need more than Your stuff—I need You. I know where we are going next—the Promised Land—and we will not make it without Your presence. Lord, we need You in an even deeper way than before." This is what hungering for holiness really means—recognizing your need for more of God in your life. Matthew 5:6 says, "Blessed are those who hunger and thirst for righteousness, for they shall be filled." In other words,

There is a difference between having the Holy Spirit at salvation and being full of the Holy Spirit.

God gets excited about people who hunger and thirst for Him. There is a difference between having the Holy Spirit at salvation and being full of the Holy Spirit—fully operating in His power and gifts. I am not arguing for a second work of the Spirit, but I am saying that if you do not have a hunger for the Holy Spirit it is possible to be saved but not full.

I know I am right about this, because when the early Church chose deacons, the apostles gave them this advice: "Therefore, brethren, seek out from among you seven men . . . full of the Holy Spirit" (Acts 6:3). They were all "brethren," they were all saved, but they weren't all full. If everyone in the Church had it all, they wouldn't have had to look very hard to find men who were full of the Holy Spirit. But the apostles said "seek out," which means to choose carefully.

You may have joined the church, but if all you have is a religion and not a hunger for holiness, you are not filled with His Spirit. And if you are not filled, you will not function in the power of God. Let me see if I can make this plain for you.

I have always had a terrible habit of driving my car until the tank was nearly empty and the "low fuel" warning light came on. I would ride around in my car on $1.50 in gas. And I didn't fill up until I was back down on empty, and the warning light was on. Later on I learned that running on fumes is not good for the car; my car runs better when it's full.

An interesting thing used to happen to my car when I drove around with the "low fuel" warning light on. If I turned a corner, the gas would slosh around and get away from the hole that goes down to the fuel pump, and the car would lose power, like it was running out of gas—chuga-chuga-chuga. Then when I got straight again the gas evened out, and it would pick up again—vroom! I would go around another corner and the gas would get away from the hole again and lose power—chuga-chuga-chuga. Then I would straighten out and it would come back up—vroom!

That is what happens in your spiritual life when you are not full of the Holy Spirit. You are riding along pretty well, going to church, doing your religious thing. But then you hit a curve in your life, and because you are not full—chuga-chuga-chuga—you have no power to handle it when you get fired, or when your kids are going crazy, or when some other

But how do you get full? First—you've got to hunger!

crisis occurs. But if you are full of the Holy Spirit, even when the curves of life come, you have power.

But how do you get full? The first step is, you've got to hunger. Hunger means thirsting for Him. It means praying without ceasing. It means fasting regularly. It means seeking to be in His presence. It means seeking a God encounter. It means letting go of everything that gets in the way of a fresh move of God in your life.

One of the biggest hindrances in our lives is hanging around people who have no hunger for God. "Do not be deceived: 'Evil company corrupts good habits'" (1 Cor. 15:33). The people you hang around with can hinder you from going deeper in God. Moses went up on the mountain to make this request and it may be that you and I need to get alone and seek God by ourselves if we are ever going to grow.

Hunger for holiness is not just about getting alone with God but it is also having an expectation when you come into His presence. Having an expectation means that you believe something is going to happen when you're in His presence.

If you are someone who has a hunger for holiness, your spirit will never get old . . .

I was playing golf one day and I met an 83-year-old man who rides a motorcycle, plays golf and skis. He said to me, "Listen, young man, I am not old."

I said, "Yes sir, you are not old." (What else could I say?)

He said, "Let me tell you why I am not old. I am

not under any illusions—I am 83 years old. But that is not old. Old is when you stop expecting."

He's right—old is when you get up thinking you have got it all together, when you think you can't learn anything else, when you stop expecting something. And I don't want my spirit to get old. But I believe that if you are someone who has a hunger for holiness, your spirit will never get old, no matter what your age, because there is always something more available in God. And once you have a hunger for holiness, and begin moving from visitation to habitation, you can expect a lot of things—such as revelation and mystery.

Revelation and Mystery

Revelation and mystery are found in Exodus 33:19–20: "Then He said, 'I will make all My goodness pass before you, and I will proclaim the name of the LORD before you. I will be gracious to whom I will be gracious, and I will have compassion on whom I will have compassion.' But He said, 'You cannot see My face; for no man shall see Me, and live.'" God said, "I will show you some things, but some things you cannot see."

This passage bothers me, because earlier, in verse 11, it says, "So the LORD spoke to Moses face to face." And yet, in verse 20, God says, "You can't see My face." Now this is where some of your friends who don't come to church, who just read the Bible quickly in passing, will say, "See? The Bible contradicts itself." On the one hand, He says He speaks face to face, and on the other hand, He says, "You can't see My face."

Is there a problem here? At first I thought it must be a different word in the Hebrew, so I looked it up. The same word for "face"—*paw-neem*—is in both verse 11 and in verse 20. I said, "Oh, my goodness, maybe this is a contradiction!" But I did some further study and found out that the phrase "face to face" is not meant to be literal. It is an expression found constantly in the Old Testament. It means "a clear verbal articulation, without vision or need of interpretation."

A lot of times God would speak to someone in the Old Testament, but in a vision, a symbol, a metaphor. It would need to be interpreted by a prophet. But when He spoke "face to face," it is like when Jacob in Genesis 32:30 named the place he was at Peniel ("face of God") because, he said, "I have seen God face to face." It means it was clear, familiar articulation—no symbols that needed to be interpreted. It means what "face" means in verse 20—the weight of glory, the full manifestation of God.

If you are filled with the Holy Spirit, you love God, and are doing well, you probably think this passage is not talking to you. You're probably thinking, *This is* talking to folks who have to get deeper in God, who don't want to pray; they really need to hear this. If so, you've missed the whole point.

When Moses asked for this deeper revelation, he already had a good relationship with God. I don't care how holy you think you are right now—there is always more to God. And one of the reasons good Christians and good churches stop growing is that they get comfortable in what God did before. You've missed it if you're saying, "God blessed me last year; God did something through me two years ago; I talked with God; I know I am spiritual." I am not doubting that, but it's like that Janet Jackson song—"What Have You Done Lately?" I know He has been good to you, but what about right now?

I don't care how holy you think you are right now— there is always more to God.

There is a sense in which Moses was saying, "Lord, I thank You for what we have, but I know there is more to You." God says to Moses, "I can show you some things, but I can't show you everything. I am going to allow My goodness to pass by you." And in Exodus 34:6–7, God passes by and calls out His name. God was saying, "I am going to show you My nature and My character. I am going to expose you to what I am all about, to who I am."

In his book *Gift and Giver: The Holy Spirit for Today*,[3] Dr. Craig Keener says that God's glory can be summarized as being full of covenant love and covenant faithfulness. In other words, when He passed by, it was full of grace and truth. You need to put a bookmark there. God exposes Moses to a new dimension of *who He is*.

Every time God gives a new name for Himself it is given because another dimension of His nature and character has been revealed. We call Him Jehovah-Jireh (the God who provides) because He revealed to Abraham on the mountain that He would provide. We call Him Jehovah-Nissi (the God who delivers) because He delivered Moses and the children of Israel from the Amorites. We call Him Jehovah-Shalom (the God of peace) because Gideon found out that as long as he had the peace of God, he had victory over the Midianites. Every time we get a new name for God in the Bible it is a new revelation of His nature.

God wants to show you more about who He is, but only if you are hungry for Him.

That is what God wants to give you—a new revelation of Himself. God wants to let you in on what He is doing in your life and in the world. God wants to show you more about who He is, but only if you are hungry for Him and faithful to what He has already shown you. At the point you tell God "no" is the point you stop getting revelation.

Faithfulness Is the Key

God will not show you the next thing that He has for you if you have not been faithful to what He has already shown you. Remember, it was forty years before Abraham found out He was Jehovah-Jireh. There were other things in Abraham's life that he had to be faithful to before God could entrust him with the Isaac experience, so that he could find out he is Jehovah-Jireh. If you want to know more about God, you better be faithful to what you already know. If you want to go deeper in God, you better start doing what you know He has already told you to do.

Maybe you want to move from visitation to habitation, but you already know what God is demanding of you and you don't want to do it. You are fighting it. You know He wants you to stay away from that guy or that girl, or go to the mission field, or get back to reading His Word and praying. But you keep saying, "I'm not going to do it." Then you turn around and say, "Lord, what is Your will?" You know what

His will is, and until you do what He has already told you to do, He can't expose you to the next level in your life.

God wants to show you many things, but as He said to Moses, "No, not My face." This speaks of the imperfect knowledge that you and I have of God, even on our best theological days. You can't handle all of His glory. You can't handle everything He knows and everything He is. Paul says in First Corinthians 13 that we see in a mirror, dimly. Deuteronomy 29:29 says that the secret things belong to the LORD our God, but those things which are revealed belong to us and to our children forever. Revelation 10:4 says that when seven thunders had uttered their voices John was about to write, but he heard a voice from heaven telling him to seal up those things which the seven thunders uttered and write them not.

Every time I think I've got God all together, in my neat little box, He breaks out of it every time.

In other words, there is a tension between revelation and mystery; there are some things that God says we can't know and can't handle. And those of us who are spiritually mature and growing are "holding the mystery of the faith with a pure conscience" (1 Tim. 3:9). We are not shaken by the fact that some things about God we can know and some remain mystery.

I may think I understand the Trinity and the Virgin Birth, but at some level these doctrines elude my understanding. I understand that God can heal, but I don't know why He doesn't do it all the time. I understand that God has all power, but I don't fully understand why He lets some things happen. I understand why I am baptized and why I take Communion, why I believe in anointing with oil, why I lay on hands; but every time I think I've got God all together, wrapped up in my wonderful theological package, He breaks out of it every time, because God is bigger than any of my theological or philosophical postulations.

And you know what? I don't want a God I can figure out! I am comfortable with a God whose ways are higher than my ways, whose thoughts are higher than my thoughts (Isa. 55:8–9). Why? Because I am a finite man dealing with infinite reality. If I have a finite god whom I have fully figured out, then when my finite self with my well-figured-out finite god bumps into the harsh, infinite realities of this world, they are bound to overwhelm me. If my God is no bigger than my own thought processes and I can't figure out what I am dealing with, then I am in trouble.

But I've got a God who is bigger than any problem, and higher than anything I can deal with. Whatever comes up against me, it is still under God's feet. And even though I don't know about tomorrow, I know *who* holds tomorrow. As long as I know that I've got a God whose ways and thoughts are higher than mine, who knows more than I know and who loves me, then I don't care what happens tomorrow. I know that God will be with me and He can handle it.

> *We'll never get too deep to find out something new, because Jeremiah says that His mercies are new every morning.*

And that's why I never get too old for Bible study, or too saved for prayer meeting. We'll never get too deep to find out something new, because Jeremiah says that His mercies are new every morning. Every day, there is something new to know about God. And so I am all right with the tension between revelation and mystery.

The Revelation Is in Jesus, the Christ

This story about Moses was written to teach us that everything is available in Christ Jesus. Christ is represented in the text in two places. First, we understand Him to be the Rock—"Rock of Ages, cleft for me, let me hide myself in Thee." The Lord told Moses to stand on the rock while His glory passed by, then

He put Moses in a cleft of the rock and covered him with His hand while He passed. In other words, God said to Moses, "If you are going to be exposed to what I am going to show you, you have to be in a position to handle it. Get in the cleft of the rock, where I can put My hand on you."

Being in Jesus Christ is what opens us to the possiblities that are in God.

God cannot expose you to who He is and you cannot be in right relationship with God without being in the Rock of Ages—Jesus, the Christ. Being in Jesus Christ is what opens us to the possibilities that are in God. It opens us up to a right relationship with God, where we can learn about God. But even more than that, it opens us up to the glory of God. Thirteen centuries later, John wrote, "In the beginning was the Word, and the Word was with God, and the Word was God. And the Word became flesh and dwelt among us. And we beheld His glory, the glory as the only begotten of the Father, full of grace and truth" (John 1:1, 14).

The wording of John 1:14 is in direct relationship to the wording of Exodus 33. In other words, what Moses saw in part thirteen centuries ago is now available to you and me in full color, and His name is

Jesus. Jesus is the full revelation of God and the glory of God. Jesus is the Lamb of God, the Son of God, the Word of God. Jesus is God with us. And if you want to move deeper in God, you have to be in Jesus, the Christ.

That's why Jesus said, "If you have seen Me, you have seen the Father" (John 14:9). In other words, if you want to know who God is, take a good look at Jesus. Jesus said, "Have I been with you this long and still you ask Me, 'Show us the Father'?" The Father's full glory is revealed in Jesus, the Christ. So if you want to move from visitation to habitation, you have to move into Jesus, the Christ.

But after you have a right relationship with Jesus, the Christ, don't just join the church, sit down and wait for heaven! It's one thing to join and another thing to grow. You need to have a hunger for holiness; in other words, you ought to come to church with some expectations. You ought to expect to experience God, and leave the meeting wanting to take God with you. But that's not all—if you want to move from visitation to habitation, you have to make up your mind that you don't want to play church, that you

One day you will find that you have grown from an "I believe" religion to an "I know" faith.

want to be serious about your spirituality, that you want to be concerned about being Christ-like.

As you move from visitation to habitation, one day you will find that you have grown from an "I believe" religion to an "I know" faith. Fifteen years ago, I would have told you that I believe He will make a way out of no way, that He will be there when I need Him, that He'll fight my battles and rock me in the cradle of His love. I've had a few years since then; I've had a few battles and a few trials since then. I don't say "I believe" any longer, because I know He'll do it! I don't just believe, I know He'll make a way out of no way. I know He'll be there when I need Him. I know He'll be bread when I'm hungry and water when I'm thirsty. I know He is a Father to the fatherless and a Friend to the friendless. I know if my friends run out on me and my family forsakes me, He'll be there—I know He will!

Hallelujah! I know, I know, I know! I am moving from visitation to habitation. And that's what God wants of you. He wants you to grow hungry for holiness, to come to grips with the tension between revelation and mystery, and to be firmly rooted in Jesus, the Christ. He wants to take you deeper, and you can't do that by yourself. It requires a relationship with God and being part of the household of faith—part of a nurturing faith community that will teach the Word of God and nurture you in your walk with God.

This chapter was written to remind you that we are on a journey. This journey will take you deeper into God if you desire to go there. One of the greatest breakthroughs in my life came when I was willing to put down my previous traditions, education and experiences and just let God speak to my heart. While I am not an advocate of blind faith or borrowed and canned religion, I know that only when you have that experience where you acknowledge to God that you need Him more that anything else in your life—only then will you find new dimensions of God and move from Visitation to Habitation.

Discussion Questions

1. What habits or practices in your life might make God respond, "You're getting too big for that"?
2. What is the relationship between growing deeper in God and surrendering your life to God?
3. What does the author say is needed before a person can be filled with the Holy Spirit?
4. Why do we often "plateau" in our Christian life? What can we do to move on to the next level?
5. What is the role of faithfulness in growing deeper in Christ?
6. How do we keep a Christ-centered approach to Christian growth?

Key Verses

Exodus 33:18   Exodus 33:19–20

Hebrews 6:1–2   Exodus 34:6–7

Matthew 5:6   Isaiah 55:8–9

John 1:1, 14

THREE

You Can't Turn Around Now

John Bunyan's classic Christian novel, *Pilgrim's Progress,* is an allegory about the pilgrimage of a Christian. It talks about how one goes from faith to trial to greater faith to greater trial. It shows how the Christian life is one of obstacles and triumphs, and it helps us recognize that on this Christian journey we don't stay in one place—it's a pilgrimage.

Another book with the same emphasis is a wonderful autobiography by Dr. Jeremiah Wright, Sr. entitled *The Pilgrimage of a Pastor.*[4] He writes about his life as the pastor of the Grace Baptist Church in Philadelphia, Pa. In this book Dr. Wright writes about what it felt like to be a young man coming to the city from a small town in Virginia, and some of the challenges he faced. He writes about the challenge of balancing family responsibilities, academic pursuits, and pastoral ministry. And he writes about his vision for Grace Church, how at times he wrestled with his call, and how he faced obstacles and yet had victory.

> *The Christian life is a journey of ups and downs, ins and outs, appointments and disappointments.*

I encourage you to read these two books, simply to be reminded that, although you have trials in your life, you can still have life, and that more abundantly. The Christian life is a journey of ups and downs, ins and outs, appointments and disappointments. The paradox of this is that there are a whole lot of twist and turns on this thing we call the straight and narrow path!

Everyone who has truly decided to follow Jesus Christ will experience what St. John of the Cross called a "dark night of the soul," and what Henry Blackaby calls a "crisis of faith." [5] In other words, God stretches us beyond ourselves. It is uncomfortable, but it is necessary if you are going to grow in Christ.

The process looks like this: You are at one place in life, and then God initiates a launch sequence in your life—He gives you a pro- phetic word, or a prompt- ing in your spirit, or a vi- sion. God lets you know what He wants you to do and what He wants to happen. Then you need faith. Faith calls you to ac-

A crisis of faith is a bump in the road that will either turn you around or take you higher.

tion. God's promises always come with the expecta- tion that your faith is going to go into action.

However, when you go into action, that's when the problems begin to occur! There will always be an obstacle—something that causes that crisis of faith Blackaby talks about. You will bump up against some- thing that requires you to hold on and learn some- thing new about God and yourself. This is never com- fortable.

When I talk about a person who is having a crisis of faith, I don't mean someone who is out of the will of God—someone who isn't doing right and is catch- ing hell as a result. That's not what I am talking about. I am talking about *you*—a saint who loves the Lord. You received a promise from the Lord and you are following it, and now you have bumped into some- thing that is challenging you. Your old belief system does not have enough to move you into the next season that God has for your life.

A crisis of faith is a bump in the road that will either turn you around or take you higher. A crisis of faith is when life presents you with a situation that will be a defining moment in your life. A crisis of faith is when you hit that place in the will of God that if God doesn't do it, it won't be done; and quite frankly, you are not comfortable with that. You can't turn around now.

God has been too good to you; He has brought you too far; He's done too much for you. Even though you don't like where you are and even though it's difficult, you can't turn around now. I want to give you a few reasons why you can't turn around now, to encourage you in your season of crisis.

The children of Israel had a crisis of faith when they came out of Egypt. This was their first real test. They were stuck in between two mountain ranges and the Red Sea, with Pharaoh and his army coming to kill them.

> And when Pharaoh drew near, the children of Israel lifted their eyes, and behold, the Egyptians marched after them. So they were very afraid, and the children of Israel cried out to the LORD. Then they said to Moses, "Because there were no graves in Egypt, have you taken us away to die in the wilderness? Why

have you so dealt with us, to bring us up out of Egypt? Is this not the word that we told you in Egypt, saying, 'Let us alone that we may serve the Egyptians'? For it would have been better for us to serve the Egyptians than that we should die in the wilderness."

And Moses said to the people, "Do not be afraid. Stand still, and see the salvation of the LORD, which He will accomplish for you today. For the Egyptians whom you see today, you shall see again no more forever. The LORD will fight for you, and you shall hold your peace." (Ex. 14:10–14)

Moses basically said, "We can't turn back now." If you are trapped in a moment of crisis like this, God is going to show you something in this moment that is going to change your understanding of who you are and of what God has for you. He is going to protect you—but you can't turn around. I want to give you four reasons why.

1. *The Devil Wants You Back*

One reason you can't turn around is because *the devil wants you to turn around*. That's what this whole thing is about—Satan is not happy with your growth. Satan is not pleased with your praise. He will not give up without a fight; he is not going to "just kiss and say good-bye." Your deliverance makes him mad.

Joining the church does not exempt you from trouble; in fact, your deliverance is what is causing the attack in your life. My father used to say, "If you are not bumping into the devil every now and then, it must be because you are walking with him." If you never have any attacks, if you're never dealing with anything difficult in your life, you must be walking with the devil.

> *If you are not bumping into the devil every now and then, it must be because you are walking with him.*

Remember, after Pharaoh let the children of Israel go, he decided to go after them and get them back. Satan does not give up his strong hold on your life without a fight. Attacks will usually be right at your point of deliverance and at the source of your ministry power. You may have been set free from a personal habit or from some ways of doing things, but now it seems like that very thing you thought you were free from is coming back at you. Satan is throwing it all in your face, in ways that you never thought would happen.

When I was in college, the Lord convicted me of a number of personal habits. What is interesting is that when I began to walk in new convictions Satan opened up new and even more enticing opportunities for me to do my old dirt. The very areas where I had authentically experienced deliverance began to be the very areas where I experienced more intense temptation. Have you ever experienced a personal breakthrough, only to then face a very serious temptation in that area of your life? Don't be surprised—it is just Pharoah /Satan trying to get you to come back to Egypt/hell.

He will also attack at the source of your ministry power. Have you ever tried to help somebody else's marriage, and found that your marriage comes under attack? You try to help somebody with raising their child, and your own child starts acting up. You try to help somebody out financially, and Satan tries to attack your money.

I've learned to recognize these situations for what they really are—Satan trying to deceive and destroy us at our very source of joy and power. I can't turn around now, because that would put me back in the hands of the one who wants to kill me. Pharaoh was not bearing down on the children of Israel at the Red Sea so that he could say, "Listen, you guys—come on back to Egypt! I'll take much better care of you." No— he was coming to kill!

Satan is also coming to kill. Why does Satan want to kill you? Because you are a fine, sanctified, Spirit-filled believer. You are a threat to the kingdom of darkness and he is ready to take you out at all costs. If you were no threat he would leave you alone, but now that you are saved and filled, and walking in the right path, he is coming after you.

You can't turn back, because that's exactly what he wants you to do. If he can get you to turn back this time, then every time you try to do something for God he is going to turn you back. If you run every time trouble comes, then you are going to be running for the rest of your life. Once Satan figures out that all he has to do is send trouble, then he'll send it by the truckload. "All I've got to do to get him running is just send a little trouble his way, and then he'll back off. All I've got to do to get her to stop praising is send a little trouble; that will shut her up."

It was always God's intention that the children of Israel be in the land of the Canaanites . . .

2. *God Wants Us Out of Egypt*

A second reason we can't turn back is because *God wants us out of Egypt.* God's destiny for the children of Israel was not in Egypt. They had been there 400 years and now they had to get out. Egypt is bondage; it is sin and low living. Egypt is out of the will of God.

And Egypt is also joylessness. God does not intend you to be unhappy all the time. There is something wrong if you are always frowning and finding fault; that is not the Spirit of God. Egypt is just not where God wants you to be.

The Promised Land is the land of Canaan: "And it shall be, when the LORD brings you into the land of the Canaanites, as He swore to you and your fathers, and gives it to you . . ." (Ex. 13:11). It was always God's intention that the children of Israel be in the land of the Canaanites, not in Egypt. God wants you to reach your Canaan potential. Self-actualization and self-fulfillment are in Canaan; God's will and destiny for your life are in Canaan. Canaan is a place of fruitfulness, contentment, abundance. Canaan is a place of high praise and worship, a place of significant relationships and a deeper walk with God. Canaan is a place where your ministry bears fruit and blesses others, a place where you enjoy life and have it more abundantly.

Don't hyper-focus on the abundant life the way some flighty, materialistic Christians do. But understand that God wants you to enjoy life. He does not intend that your theme song be "I'm Climbing Up the Rough Side of the Mountain." God does not intend for you to live beaten and burdened down. God intends for you to live victoriously. And you can't do that if you are still in Egypt.

As long as you are in Egypt you can't experience the full joy of what God has for you, even if Egypt was legitimately good for you in another season. Remember, the story of the children of Israel does not begin with Moses going to the Promised Land; it begins with Abraham. The promise was given to Abraham that his descendants would inherit the land of the Canaanites. Abraham had Isaac, Isaac had Jacob, and Jacob had twelve sons, including Joseph. Joseph was sold into slavery in Egypt, and when he interpreted Pharoah's dream about a seven-year famine he was appointed second-in-command in Egypt. While Joseph was alive, Egypt was a good place for the children of Israel; but after he died, "there arose a new king over Egypt, who did not know Joseph" (Ex. 1:8), and that season was over.

I am suggesting that there are periods in your life when God allows certain things to go on, but when He is ready to take you to another level He says, "It's time to get rid of that; it will no longer be allowed."

Even if Egypt was good for you at another season, it is time to get out now. It worked for a while, but now it's time to move on. It was the permissive will of God for a season, but the ultimate will of God is in Canaan. In Acts 17:30, Paul says there was a time when we used to worship idols and God "winked" at it (as the King James says), or overlooked it, but He is not winking at it any longer! Paul is expressing the concept of the progressive revelation of God in history—the idea that God reveals new truth in new eras and, as a result, places new demands upon His people. He is also implying the concept of progressive sanctification in the individual believer—the idea that God leads us on to deeper and deeper levels of holiness and purity. I am suggesting that there are periods in your life when God allows certain things to go on, but when He is ready for you to move on He says, "It's time to get rid of that; it will no longer be allowed."

God gave you grace in the issue of finances for a while, but now He is not winking at your lack of trusting Him by failing to tithe. It's time to move on. Up to now God has not dealt with that questionable relationship of yours, for whatever reason. Now He is ready to take you somewhere—maybe a new area of ministry—and that person can't go with you. God allowed you to function that way for a while, but now that is Egypt, and you've got to move on.

In fact, if you don't move on, that which was good will now be bad for you. Have you ever tried to go back to some sinful habit you gave up when you got saved? Have you ever said to yourself, "I'll try it just one more time"? You are saved, you love the Lord, you go to church, but you thought you'd try it just once more. You'll find that it doesn't work; it doesn't feel right. The Holy Spirit is inside you now, and He's grieved—every time you try it, He says, "That ain't us no more." It's because it is Egypt, and God wants us out of there.

> *Once God declares an area off-limits to you, if you go back to it, it won't be like it used to be— it will be worse.*

But you don't need to go back to Egypt to know that it's not good for you; the Lord too taught this principle. When Jesus healed that man at the Pool of Bethesda He said, "Sin no more, lest a worse thing come upon you" (John 5:14). Once God declares an area off-limits to you, if you go back to it, it won't be like it used to be—it'll be worse. You'll have no joy or peace if you keep going back. You can't turn back now. God has brought you too far.

3. *God Wants Egypt Out of You*

The third reason you can't turn back is because *God wants Egypt out of you.* The Israelites had been in slavery for 400 years, and you don't stay in something that long without it getting into you. This is why, at the first sign of trouble (Pharaoh's army closing in on them), the children of Israel said to Moses, "Is this not the word that we told you in Egypt, saying, 'Let us alone that we may serve the Egyptians'? For it would have been better for us to serve the Egyptians than that we should die in the wilderness" (Ex. 14:12).

This was their problem: they still thought of Egypt as a place that was good for them! God said to them, "Not only do I have to get you out of there, I've got to get 'there' out of you." Your deliverance is not just about your geography, but also your psychology and your sociology.

But before we talk about deliverance, let's go back a few verses and see how the children of Israel got into the predicament of being trapped by the Red Sea with the Egyptians bearing down on them.

> Now the LORD spoke to Moses, saying: "Speak to the children of Israel, that they turn and camp before Pi Hahiroth, between Migdol and the sea, opposite Baal Zephon; you shall camp before it by the sea. For Pharaoh will say of the children of Israel, 'They are bewildered by the land; the wilderness has closed them in.'" (Ex. 14:1–3)

Why were the children of Israel stuck at the Red Sea between two mountains? Because God sent them there! He deliberately told them to camp in a place where they would be trapped with no place to run. Wait a minute—couldn't He have sent them somewhere else? Let's check the record: "Then it came to pass, when Pharaoh had let the people go, that God did not lead them by way of the land of the Philistines, although that was near; for God said, 'Lest perhaps the people change their minds when they see war, and return to Egypt'" (Ex. 13:17).

God was orchestrating this whole thing. He said to Himself, "If I take them out of Egypt and through the land of the Philistines, they'll be walking into a fight. These people still have a slave mentality; they are not ready for war. In fact, even Moses will probably turn around if he sees that! I've got to put them in a situation that will help them see who I really am—a situation that is stressful enough that they call on Me but not so stressful that they give up on Me."

> *If I am at an impasse because I am following the will of God, I must trust that He can get me through.*

My grandma always said, "He knows just how much I can bear." He knows what I can deal with. If I am at an impasse because I am following the will of God, I must trust that He can get me through. If God knows I can't handle it, He will protect me from it. But if God knows I *need* to handle it, He will set it up, but be on my side.

God knew that war with the Philistines would be too much for them. But He also knew that they needed some pressure that would teach them who God is, and knock the "Egypt" out of them. So He set up the predicament—but He was on their side.

This puts "turning around" in a whole new light, doesn't it? If I understand that the predicament I am in is orchestrated by God, then Pharaoh's army is not my biggest problem. Because if God orchestrated this, then turning around means I'm fighting God. So now I have a choice: I can keep going forward—which is difficult, but at least I am only fighting the devil, and God is on my side. Or, I can turn around—but then I'm fighting God, and who is going to help me? I'd rather fight the devil, knowing that God is a God who "makes a way out of no way"—knowing that nothing is too hard for God. So I can't turn around now.

God set up this whole thing with Pharaoh's army because He knew that once the Israelites got through it, they would learn a few things. Have you ever been through a hard time and learned some things about God

I used to have an "I believe" Christianity; now I have an "I know" Christianity.

that nobody can take from you? Has God ever blessed you? Has God ever taken you through things that other folks did not survive? And now you know.

I used to have an "I believe" Christianity; now I have an "I know" Christianity. I used to say, "I believe He will make a way." Now I say, "I know, because I've walked with Him and He has brought me from a mighty long way." God not only wants to get you out of Egypt, He wants to get Egypt out of you.

There are some things about God, and what God can do, that are just not debatable. In fact, there is a historic praise song from the African-American church that sums up how I feel. It says, "You can't make me doubt Him, 'cause I know too much about Him. You can't make me doubt Him in my heart."

4. *God Wants to Bring Out the Best in You*

The final reason why you can't turn around now is because *God wants to bring out the best in you.* Remember what God said to Moses at the burning bush:

> So I have come down to deliver them out of the hand of the Egyptians, and to bring them up from that land to a good and large land, to a land flowing with milk and honey, to the place of the Canaanites and the Hittites and the Amorites and the Perizzites and the Hivites and the Jebusites. (Ex. 3:8)

That passage says that the Promised Land is flowing with milk and honey—it has everything you need and want. But it also has Hittites and Amorites— pagan people that are living there and don't want to leave. God is saying to them, "When you go into the Promised Land you are going to have to fight to get it. You are going to have to do some battle."

Earlier God had them avoid the land of the Philistines because He wanted them protected from battle. They weren't ready for battle then, although

Nothing solid and valuable comes without a fight.

someday they would be. He was getting them ready for the time they would have to battle, because nothing good or lasting comes easily and quickly. Nothing solid and valuable comes without a fight.

But at this point they are not ready to fight, so God orchestrates a confrontation to get the "Egypt" out of them—the stuff that keeps them from being able to go to the next level. This also produces something in them that is necessary for the next level. In this confrontation God gets some junk out, but He puts some good stuff in them too, so they'll be ready to march into the Promised Land.

Remember the conversation I had with my coffee cup? Well, I had another one of those kitchen conversations, and it wasn't with a cup, but with a tea bag. I was sitting there Friday night drinking my tea, and the tea bag said, "Alyn, I really got jealous last week when I saw you talking to the coffee cup. I really wanted you to ask me something about the sermon."

I said, "But the coffee cup had a wonderful illustration about journeying and I appreciated it."

"I understand that," he said. "But I heard that you were preaching about the children of Israel getting stuck there between the Red Sea and those two mountains, and I think you need to tell the people my story."

I said, "What in the world, Mr. Tea Bag, do you have to say to my congregation?"

He said, "You have to tell the people that tea bags and Christians have a whole lot in common."

"What in the world do you mean?" I asked.

He said, "Neither one of us are any good until we are put in some hot water. Put me in some hot water and watch my flavor come out. Put me in some hot water and watch me become all that I can be."

If you are in hot water, it may be because God is bringing out the flavor in you.

If you are in hot water, it may be because God is bringing out the flavor in you. God is getting ready to bless you, to do a special thing in your life. But you have to hold on, and when it looks like you can't hold on any longer, watch God perform a miracle. Watch Him open up the Red Sea; watch yourself go through in victory; watch your enemies come under your feet. Just hold on.

I've learned that when I get into hot water, God is just making something beautiful out of my life. I've learned how to praise Him in the midst of trouble, because in the time of trouble He will hide me. So when trouble comes, start praising Him and giving Him the glory!

We can't turn back now; He has brought us too far. Maybe you have not yet accepted Christ, but He has been good to you anyhow. And He has been leading your life so that you would *come* to accept Him. It is not a coincidence that you are reading this—on this very day. God wants to speak to your life right now. He wants to make sense out of your journey. Or maybe you know Christ as your Savior but you are almost ready to give up on church, to give up on God. You can't turn around now. You need to be in a place where your faith will be supported and where you will be developed. The prevenient grace of God has brought you to this moment. You can't turn around now.

Discussion Questions

1. What does the author mean by a "crisis of faith"? Have you ever found yourself in this situation?
2. What kinds of attacks does the devil send our way? What is his strategy?
3. What does "Egypt" represent in the life of the Christian?
4. Why does God orchestrate difficulties in our lives?
5. How can troubled times bring out the best in us? What do we need to remember in these times?

Key Verses

Exodus 13:17	Exodus 14:1–3
Exodus 14:10–14	Acts 17:30

FOUR

There Is Always Another River

Life is a journey. Life is full of appointments and disappointments. Life is full of fun and failure. The key to life is to enjoy the journey, face the challenges, and keep on moving.

One of the challenges that I come across as a pastor is that far too many people in the church believe that at some point in the Christian's journey the challenges will stop. The reality, however, is that there will always be another river to cross. There will always be another mountain to climb, another challenge to face. The thing we have to remember is that the deeper in God we go the more faith and action God will require of us on the journey.

Earlier we discussed the crossing of the Red Sea by Moses and the children of Israel. In that crossing God basically said to the children of Israel, "Just stand back and watch Me work." It was one of those experiences with God that grow our faith and deepen our walk.

There is now another river to cross—in the book of Joshua, chapter 3. At this river more action and faith are required on the part of the children of Israel to cross this obstacle. Let me summarize this chapter for you.

The children of Israel find themselves blocked by another body of water, but this time it is not the Red Sea; it is the Jordan River. It is forty years after the crossing of the Red Sea; Moses has died, and Joshua has been given leadership of the Israelites. They are no longer slaves; these people have been transformed by forty years in the wilderness. They have seen the hand of the Lord fight for them; they have felt the hand of the Lord chastise them for faithlessness and reward them for faithfulness. They are a people who know about God now. They have learned that He is Jehovah Nissi (the LORD our Deliverer), because He delivered them from the Amorites and Og, the king of Bashan (Num. 21:21–35). They have seen how, for forty years, He did not let their clothes or shoes wear out. They are the people who ate manna in the wilderness. They are the people who have the law, the covenant, the ark of the covenant.

The Israelites waited at the Jordan for three days; then the officers went throughout the camp to tell them it was time to cross over. They followed the ark, but at a distance, and the interesting thing is that this time the water didn't part for them until they put their feet in it. Forty years ago they didn't know much about God, so God just parted the Red Sea; there was no fear to battle and no faith to exercise—it just opened up. But at the Jordan, God was saying, "Step out there in faith, and when you step out I will meet you there." That's what you have to do.

If you are a mature Christian, then I want you to realize that you've moved past the Red Sea experiences. Maybe you've been walking with the Lord awhile, but you are at another impasse. You love the Lord, but you are right on the brink of the Promised Land and you are trying to get a breakthrough. You are at the Jordan, and there are five things you need to know about crossing this river.

1. *Wait for a Word*

First, you have to wait for a word. Joshua and all the Israelites camped at the Jordan for three days before the officers went through the camp and told them it was time to cross over. I don't care what you know about a situation—until you hear from the Lord it is not time to move. You may want that new job; you may think you've found the right man or woman to share your life with. You can see the Promised Land right over there—but don't move until you have heard from the Lord.

> . . . *if He is in it,*
> *it's going to work.*

You have been with the Lord long enough to know that if He is in it, it's going to work, and if He is not in it, it won't work. So don't lean on your own understanding—wait until you hear a word from the Lord. Don't get married just because you like and love each other; don't come to the altar with anybody until you have heard from the Lord that she or he ought to be your spouse.

Some people treat marriage like it is in vogue—they get married just because they like the idea of getting married. Make sure when you walk down the aisle that you are standing there with someone that you not only have *eros* love for (you think they are attractive), and *phileo* love for (you love them because they love you), and *agape* love for (the overflow of God's love in your life into their life), but also be sure that you have heard from God that this is the person He wants you to be with.

Before you do anything, make sure you hear from the Lord. What about your job, for example? What would happen if, as a pastor, I told my congregation, "There is a church down the street that has offered me $40,000 more than you are paying me, so I am leaving"? They would all say, "I knew it! All those preachers want is money." But if you were working in a secular job and another firm offered you $40,000 more, you would come to church saying, "I've been blessed—the Lord has given me a promotion!"

Whatever comes your way, you need to ask, "Did God tell me to take it?"

What's my point? It's that whether you are a pastor or not, the motivation for your life is not money. The motivation for your life is making sure you are in the will of God. Whatever comes your way, you need to ask, "Did God tell me to take it?" It is not right to go to a church just for how much they can pay. But it is also not right to take a job based on what they pay. The real issue is, did God tell you to go there? Because ultimately, if you have not heard a word from the Lord, you'd better stay where you are.

I don't know how God speaks to you—visions, an audible voice, whatever—but you'd better learn to hear a word.

Now I think I need to remind you that there is a difference between being lazy and waiting on the Lord. In Joshua 3:1, it says that the children of Israel walked from Acacia Grove to the Jordan. They didn't start waiting until they got to the Jordan. Acacia Grove is about ten miles away from the Jordan, which is a half day's journey. God did not carry them to the Jordan; they had to walk there themselves.

Then when they arrived at the Jordan, they waited on God to meet them. There are some things you have to do even while you wait. Waiting means doing what you can, with what you have, where you are, until you receive further instructions. Waiting for God means that you stay faithful to the last thing He said until you hear something new. Waiting means doing your part. If you are praying for a job, fill out an application. If you are praying for food, set your table. If you are praying for your spouse to begin to love you and act toward you in ways that meet your needs, you need to start fulfilling the Biblical role you are supposed to fulfill until he or she begins to turn around. Are you praying for a financial breakthrough?

Start tithing. Don't just sit there and wait for God to show up. Waiting means while you are there you are being faithful to what you know God has already said.

2. *Pursue His Presence*

Not only do you need to wait for a word, you need to pursue His presence. In Joshua 3:3, it says that the officers told the people, "When you see the ark of the covenant of the LORD your God, and the priests, the Levites, bearing it, then you shall set out from your place and go after it." The children of Israel were told to follow the ark, stay with the ark, not to move without the ark. The ark was a symbol of the presence of the Lord.

This is different than at the Red Sea where there was a pillar of cloud and a pillar of fire—obvious signs and wonders. This is forty years later; God has designed an ark where His presence rests and now they are following the ark. The point of the spiritual life is to be in the presence of the Lord. Not just seeking His signs and wonders, but being in His presence.

I want to be in the presence of God because then I am in the will of God. I want to experience the glory of God. The fullness of joy is in the presence of the Lord. The fullness of peace, power and provision is in the presence of the Lord. I want to be in His presence. When I come to worship, I want to experience His discernible presence. I don't know about you, but I am at a point in my life where I am not asking, "Does this tickle my flesh?" or, "Is this my cultural preference?" but, "Is God in this?" I don't need man-made manufactured religious experiences; I don't want hyped-up superficial performances; I want to be in His presence.

> *I don't want hyped-up superficial performances; I want to be in His presence.*

Not only in church, but even outside of church, I want to be in God's presence. I don't want anything on me or around me that is going to tear me away from His presence. Do you know what it feels like to be in His presence? It's what David talks about in the Twenty-third Psalm: "You anoint my head with oil; my cup runs over" (v. 5). As I am walking through the paths of righteousness, as I am going through the valley of the shadow of death, I fear no evil because the Lord is with me. Why? Because I am in His presence and He's anointing my head with oil and my cup runs over.

That's why you can keep your head when everybody else is going crazy on the job—because you are in His presence. That's why you can bless the Lord at all times and praise Him continually—because you are in His presence. That's why I love the psalm that says,

He who dwells in the secret place of the Most High
　　Shall abide under the shadow of the Almighty.
I will say of the LORD,
　　"He is my refuge and my fortress;
My God, in Him I will trust."

　　Surely He shall deliver you
From the snare of the fowler
　　And from the perilous pestilence.

He shall cover you with His feathers,
　　And under His wings you shall take refuge;
His truth shall be your shield and buckler.
　　You shall not be afraid of the terror by night,
Nor of the arrow that flies by day,
　　Nor of the pestilence that walks in darkness,
Nor of the destruction that lays waste at noonday.

　　A thousand may fall at your side,
And ten thousand at your right hand;
　　But it shall not come near you.
Only with your eyes shall you look,
　　And see the reward of the wicked.

Because you have made the LORD,
　　Who is my refuge, even the Most High,
Your dwelling place,
　　No evil shall befall you,
Nor shall any plague come near your dwelling;

For He shall give His angels charge over you,
　　To keep you in all your ways.
In their hands they shall bear you up,
　　Lest you dash your foot against a stone.

You shall tread upon the lion and the cobra,
   The young lion and the serpent
You shall trample underfoot.

"Because he has set his love upon Me,
   Therefore I will deliver him;
I will set him on high,
   Because he has known My name."
                                   (Ps. 91:1–14)

If that is what is going to happen in His presence, then I want to be there.

3. *Honor His Holiness*

The third thing we must do is honor His holiness. The Lord told the Israelites to keep a distance of about a thousand yards between them and the ark. This was to symbolize the sacredness of the ark. There ought to be an appropriate distance between man and God. But wait a minute—if that's true, what about being in His presence, about getting close? What about being intimate?

> *Getting closer to God ought to cause you to have a deeper respect and reverence for the things and people of God.*

Yes, be intimate, but don't be ignorant. Be close, but don't get common. Getting closer to God ought to cause you to have a deeper respect and reverence for the things and people of God. It is no sign of spiritual maturity to think that you can talk to people any way you want. It is not a sign of spiritual maturity to think that you can disobey, that you can treat the things of God with no respect. That's a sign of immaturity.

A friend of mine, Dr. Jason Barr of Macedonia Baptist Church in Pittsburgh, once said, "Grandma's generation accepted authority; Mama's generation questioned authority; this generation says, 'What authority?'" In our cynical world we have lost that sense of awe that should be associated with the things of God. The things and people of God are important, and you can block your blessings by getting too common in your spirituality.

The reality that you are growing in grace suggests that you should place more emphasis on personal prayer time and corporate praise. The fact that you are beginning to go deeper in God means that you should honor your spiritual leaders, and live by Biblical principles even more. We have been set free from legalistic Christianity and religious garbage, but we have not been set free to become common with the things and people of God.

Remember, I am talking about the Jordan River crossing, not the Red Sea crossing. I am talking about the person who has been walking with the Lord. There ought to be respect and reverence for the things of God. This applies to how we treat the church, how we act in the sanctuary, how we read the Word, how we address the men and women of God, and most importantly, how we treat the poor and oppressed.

This applies to how we talk about God. God is awesome; the things of God are to be revered; God is to be worshiped. "The LORD is in His holy temple. Let all the earth keep silence before Him" (Hab. 2:20). There ought to be a sense of awe and sacredness. We should not treat a church sanctuary like any old place.

The Biblical understanding is that all of life is sacred.

We live in an age where many churchgoers think of a church sanctuary as an *auditorium*, and you will even hear people sometimes refer to the congregation as an *audience*. Sometimes you can tell how much a congregation reverences a sanctuary by what they leave on the floor when the service is over. I understand a bulletin or two lying around, but *potato-chip bags*?

We ought to have some sense of honor, respect and reverence—not only on the inside, but on the outside. The Christian life is not a division of sacred and secular; the Biblical understanding is that all of life is sacred. So the issue of reverence and honoring the holiness of God is not confined to clothing and actions inside the church, or the worship experience—it is about how we live every day of our lives.

As you mature in your walk with God and begin to recognize that God has taken you over a few rivers, you will begin to realize that honoring God's holiness will affect your being able to move with God. Not honoring God will frustrate your blessing. That's the meaning of the story in First Chronicles 13:9–10, where a man named Uzza touched the ark of the covenant and died. That doesn't make sense to us in our culture; we want to make excuses for the guy. But the rule was that he was not to touch it, and he should not have been so close.

In our day, we don't understand the concept of honoring the holiness of God. But the deeper you go in God the more your worship should be real, and the more you should honor the things of God and the people of God. The more mature you become in your walk with God the more you ought to honor the holiness of God. It will frustrate your life if you don't.

4. *Sanctify Yourself*

Another thing you have to do before crossing that river is to sanctify yourself. Joshua told the people, "Sanctify yourselves, for tomorrow the LORD will do wonders among you" (Josh. 3:5). This is different than the crossing of the Red Sea, because at that time Moses simply told them to stand still, and God parted the water. But here the word to them is "Sanctify yourselves." Why?

Remember, it is forty years later, and they now have the law. There was no "sanctify yourselves" at the Red Sea because they didn't have any law—they would not have understood. They would have said, "What do you mean, sanctify ourselves? We've just come out of slavery. What law are you talking about?"

You know what the Word says . . . to get over this river, you have to start living right.

But now they know what God expects of them. And He is saying, "For this next level, you have to do some living if I am going to let you cross this river." God didn't ask you to do anything when He saved you; He just asked you to accept Him. And the Red Sea is really that type of crossing. God didn't require anything of you to get you out of the mess you were in; He just saved you. But now that you have been walking with Him for a while, He's been teaching you some things. You know what the Word says; you know what is expected of you. To get over this river, you have to start living right.

He didn't say anything about those cigarettes when He got you out of Egypt, but now that He is getting ready to take you to the Promised Land those cigarettes have got to go. He didn't say anything about who you were with when He saved you, but now that He is getting ready to elevate you that sinful relationship has got to go. He didn't say anything about what you were drinking when He picked you up and turned you around, but now He is getting ready to do a new thing and you can't have that anymore.

God wants to take you into a new season, but you have got to start living according to His will. Sin will mess you up. I know everybody deals with things—"For all have sinned and fall short of the glory of God" (Rom. 3:23)—but if you've been walking with the Lord for a while and He has revealed some things in your life, God is telling you where He wants to take you. You cannot continue to sin willfully, doing what you know He has told you He does not want you to do. You aren't at the Red Sea now, you are at the Jordan, and the next stop is the Promised Land.

I do not want this chapter to sound legalistic or puritanical. I understand that there is always a gap in every life between what we are and what we should be. I also understand that the reality is that the grace of God through the shed blood of Jesus Christ, not our good works, is the only thing that makes us right before God. However, obedience to the will of God in our lives is a prerequisite for moving deeper in your journey with God. God honors faithfulness.

If you are going into the Promised Land, God expects faithful living out of you, because He wants to use you. In the Promised Land, God wants you to be a witness. There are some people that are very gifted and talented, but God can't take them to the next level. They have gifts that will take them there, but their character won't keep them there.

> *There are some people that are gifted and talented, but God can't take them to the next level. They have gifts that will take them there, but their character won't keep them there.*

God told them to sanctify themselves because folks from Egypt will turn Canaan into Egypt if they don't get Egypt out of them. Sanctify yourself.

5. *Step Out on Faith*

You may be saying, "I am doing everything you told me to do, but the water is not parting. I have been faithful; I am honoring His holiness and pursuing His presence, but nothing is happening!" Remember, my friend, this isn't the Red Sea. Notice the difference in the instructions Joshua gave to the people:

> Behold, the ark of the covenant of the Lord of all the earth is crossing over before you into the Jordan. . . . And it shall come to pass, as soon as the soles of the feet of the priests who bear the ark of the LORD, the Lord of all the earth, shall rest in the waters of the Jordan, that the waters of the Jordan shall be cut off, the waters that come down from upstream, and they shall stand as a heap. (Josh. 3:11, 13)

At the Red Sea God just opened up the water, but at the Jordan He said, "You have to step out there." The reason He opened the Red Sea was to prove to the children of Israel what He could do. But at the Jordan, God was saying to them, "I've been with you a long time now; you know what I can do. You don't need to wait to see Me open something up for you to step out. When you put your feet in the water, I'll start to work, because I am going to meet you at your level of faith."

In other words, the previous time, at the Red Sea, God showed everything up front; this time He said, "Take Me at My word." The first time He said, "Look what I can do"; this time He said, "Remember who I am." The previous time He required nothing of the Israelites; this time He said, "Sanctify yourselves." The first time, He made a road in the sea; this time He made a superhighway.

The first time, at the Red Sea, it says that when

they walked through, the water was on each side of them, on their left and on their right. God opened up the water enough so that they could get through. But when they stepped out into the waters of the Jordan, God cut off the water at a city called Adam, about nineteen miles up the river. He dried up the river from Adam all the way down to the Salt Sea.

You think God has blessed you? You think you have seen God work? I dare you to step out on God's Word. I dare you to not walk by sight, but by faith.

You think God has blessed you? You think you have seen God work? You haven't seen anything yet! I dare you to step out on God's Word. I dare you to not walk by sight, but by faith. If God says jump, you say, "How high?" If God says walk, you say, "How far?" If God says wait, you say, "How long?" I dare you to take Him at His word. See if God won't open up a superhighway for you and bless you like you have never been blessed before.

Have you ever taken God at His word and realized that God will make a way somehow? The deeper you go in God, the wider God will open doors. The more faith you express, the farther God takes you. You can't move until you hear a word, pursue His presence, honor His holiness, and sanctify yourself.

But don't wait for everything to open up—step out in faith.

This is not self-help stuff; if you are not in Christ, these things don't apply. This is accessible to us because we are in Christ Jesus; we have been made alive by the blood of Jesus Christ. If you have not accepted Jesus Christ as your personal Lord and Savior, it is God's will that you be saved; God wants you to come. This could be your Red Sea crossing.

But maybe you are at the Jordan crossing. Maybe you are at this place in your life: You are ready to move forward, but you haven't, because you are afraid to go deep in God. Maybe you are a mature Christian—you love God—but for whatever reason, you are a nonparticipant at your local church. Maybe you used to be a strong church worker, but for some reason or other you have gotten away from that. God wants to take you deeper this year.

It is not right to say, "I am a Christian, I just don't go to church—I don't want to be bothered with that." While I recognize that there are problems with the traditional church and that many good Christians have become disillusioned with organized religion, I still want to encourage you to let the Lord lead you to a Christ-centered, Spirit-led, socially conscious church where you can carry out your covenant with God. Part of our involvement in the universal Church is played out in our commitment to a local assembly. If you have accepted Christ but you aren't carrying out your covenant, today is a good day for you to recommit your life back to God and begin your journey.

Discussion Questions

1. What is the difference between the Red Sea crossing and the Jordan crossing?
2. What should you be doing when you are waiting for the Lord?
3. How do you "pursue His presence" on a day-to-day basis? What changes could you make in your life to make this pursuit more fruitful?
4. What outward expressions of respect and honor for God's holiness do you practice? What others might you consider adopting?
5. Just as we cannot save ourselves by our own efforts, we cannot live a holy life in our own efforts. In light of this, how do we obey the command to "sanctify ourselves"?
6. What does it mean to take a step of faith? Has God shown you a step of faith that He wants you to take?

Key Verses

Joshua 3
Psalm 91:1–14

Psalm 23:5
Habakkuk 2:20

End Notes:

1. Martin Luther King, Jr., *A Knock at Midnight* (New York: Warner Books, 1998).
2. Tommy Tenny, *The God Chasers* (Shippensburg, Pa: Destiny Image, 1998).
3. Craig Keener, *Gift and Giver: The Holy Spirit for Today* (Grand Rapids: Baker, 2001).
4. Jeremiah Wright, Sr., *The Pilgrimage of a Pastor* (Atlanta: Aaron Press, 1989).
5. Henry Blackaby, *Experiencing God* (Nashville: Broadman and Holman, 1994).

This book was produced by CLC Publications. We hope it has been life-changing and has given you a fresh experience of God through the work of the Holy Spirit. CLC Publications is an outreach of CLC Ministries International, a global literature mission with work in over 50 countries. If you would like to know more about us or are interested in opportunities to serve with a faith mission, we invite you to contact us at:

CLC Ministries International
PO Box 1449
Fort Washington, PA 19034

—

Phone: (215) 542-1242
E-mail: clcmail@clcusa.org
Websites: www.clcusa.org

DO YOU LOVE GOOD CHRISTIAN BOOKS?
Do you have a heart for worldwide missions?

You can receive a FREE subscription to:

Floodtide
(CLC's magazine on global literature missions)
Order by e-mail at:

floodtide@clcusa.org
or fill in the coupon below and mail to:

P.O. Box 1449
Fort Washington, PA 19034

READ THE REMARKABLE STORY OF

the founding of

CLC INTERNATIONAL

"Any who doubt that Elijah's God still lives ought to read of the money supplied when needed, the stores and houses provided, and the appearance of personnel in answer to prayer."

—Moody Monthly

Is it possible that the printing press, the editor's desk, the Christian bookstore, and the mail order department, can glow with the fast-moving drama of an "Acts of the Apostles"?

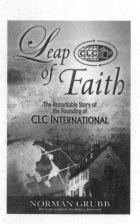

Find out, as you are carried from two people in an upstairs bookroom to a world-wide chain of Christian bookcenters, multiplied by nothing but a "shoestring" of faith and committed, though unlikely, lives.

William L. Banks

A classic devotional companion now in a new edition, *Daily Manna* is an outgrowth of a pastor's inner-city ministry which has now spanned five decades. Dr. William L. Banks leads you through the Bible from Genesis to Revelation as he inspires us to lead more godly lives though meditation on God's Word.

Make *Daily Manna* a good beginning of each new day!

Mass Market ISBN 0-87508-756-6

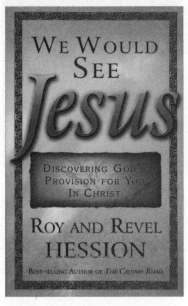

Now also in Spanish

Do you struggle with guilt or feel like God can't accept you as you are?

It's easy to forget that nothing we do will make us more acceptable to God. Jesus came to set us free to serve Him in the freshness and spontaneity of the Spirit, and to receive the ABUNDANT blessing God has for us.

Let your life be transformed as you learn to see Jesus, who is both the blessing and the way to that blessing—the means and the end.

Mass Market ISBN 958-9149-25-1

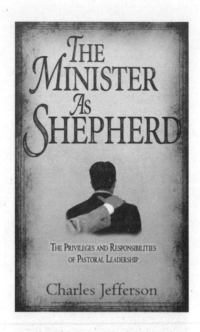

Charles E. Jefferson

"Do you have a shepherd's heart?"

In an age where too many see the pastoral ministry as obsolete, Charles Jefferson declares that it is more needed than ever, and issues a clarion call to return to the Biblical concept of the pastor as a shepherd. Jefferson takes an in-depth look at Scripture and history to explain how the shepherd model can change your paradigm of ministry.

"This book is one of perhaps a dozen in my library that I try to read again each year. It does my heart good."

Warren Wiersbe

Trade Paper ISBN 0-87508-774-4

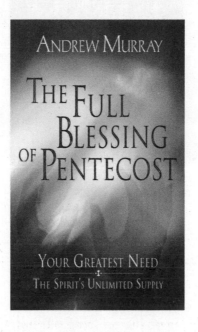

Andrew Murray

We believe it, we preach it, we strive for it—but still for many, the kind of free-flowing life in the fullness of the Spirit is more of a dream than a reality. Andrew Murray skillfully identifies the defects in faith that prevent the life-giving flow, and guides us to the Spirit's full blessing.

Let *The Full Blessing of Pentecost* show you how to find the well of living water you've been searching for.

Trade Paper ISBN 0-87508-785-X

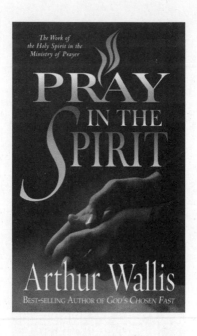

Arthur Wallis

Arthur Wallis has written a powerful book that goes beyond general principles to show the role of the Holy Spirit in the life of the praying believer. Through a pointed analysis of our spiritual and practical difficulties in prayer, Wallis shows how the Holy Spirit helps us in our weakness.

Learn how to yield yourself to Him, to allow Him to pray through you, and let the Holy Spirit lead you into "the deep things of God." When God pours out His spirit, we should expect to see a new "spirit of grace and supplication," in which "the majestic LORD will be for us a place of broad rivers and streams" (Isa. 33:21).

Trade Paper ISBN 0-87508-574-1